VINTAGE RITUALS

KJ GOFORTH

Gotham Books

30 N Gould St.
Ste. 20820, Sheridan, WY 82801

Phone: 1 (307) 464-7800

Published by Gotham Books (July 25, 2023)

ISBN: 979-8-88775-382-9 (H)
ISBN: 979-8-88775-380-5 (P)
ISBN: 979-8-88775-381-2 (E)

Breaking free is our choice
It's our will with a voice

Stifling stagnate spiritually dead
Religions flag is blood red

Atrocities grand in scale
Cowardly weasel wagging its tale

It need you place in line
Stealing all that is divine

Separation church and state
Framers nailed it no debate

Playing the hand that I was dealt
Expressing my feeling what I have felt

The mindblowing comfort deep in my soul
Guides me and tells me to let it all go

In every moment of every day
Positive focus in every way

Unconditional time stands still
Dedication and commitment paying the bill

Though it wasn't easy I've always had this trust
Life had to have some meaning under the crust

Rolling the dice must become
The reason for which I have come

Light and loving standing proud
Standing out in every crowd

Humble holding out my light
For the next one to take flight

Listen in the silence do you hear the voice
Communication close giving us a choice

Compromised or clear free to pick and choose
What a pretty dress do you like my shoes?

Focused on material afraid to look inside
Secrets we be holding off course without a guide

Butchered by betrayal terrorized in fame
Righteous on the inside vanity in vain

Building back the love each of us our own
Sovern in existence each and every bone

Please take what I give find it in yourself
Rise above the rest regenerate your health

It will take the strength courage and some change
Freedom has a cost grind away the chains

Live your truth inlove be the best you can
Get out in the sun get yourself a tan

Last of all get honest a feeling that's been lost
Walk out of the forest to the sunlight and defrost

Bent over crying hands to the head
Feeling alone like I am dead

Time spent confused darkness surrounds
Where is my family and their beautiful sounds

Isolated and trapped out on a limb
Walking the plank sink or learn swim

Crashing of waves turbulent seas
Lost on an ocean violent the breeze

Chaos ensues how can it be
This should be easy I should be free

All is not just all is not fair
All is the witness all is the dare

Laughing at liars punking the punks
Greeting the grateful discernment for drunks

Bitter bastards pack your bags
Wring out your bloody negative nags

Lay your weary head to rest
Change is coming you've passed the test

Forgetting self remembered soul
Letting it out letting it go

Restricted and confined far too long
Energy rising sing my song

On top of the world beyond the stars
Streaming lights classic cars

Turning keys discovering
Not everything is as it seems

A tick a tock accurate
See our truth start livin it

Squareing off mens big lies
Settling the score patronize

Meat and potatoes vomit stew
Change is coming after you

Held back tied up drowning in goo
What is the culprit is it me is it you

Together as one is our true power
How to get there my question this hour

Complex in denial buried in lies
Power corrupt darkening eyes

Conformity casting emotional pain
For front of sickness cancerous strain

No low to low power prevails
Taking the wind out of our sails

This time is different something must change
Before humanity blows up its brains

Intelligent laughable look around
Treading on trash left on the ground

Low on respect less in its trust
Patient on life support bank account bust

Revealing achievements ignorant deeds
Blinding the children killing new seeds

Lessons learnt bridges burnt

Solitary mercenary

Spreading hope off the dope

Free of will climbed the hill

Visionary I do carry

Dreaming dreams life it seems

Letting go shadow soul

Raised from death now with breath

Confident with intent

Glowing bright through the night

Theories tested now well rested

Time to glow time to show

Breaking the rules yet here I am
On top of the world from where it began

Poised for the greatness for what's been told
Intrigued by the mysteries of our true soul

Hoisted and hung decapitation
How many times same occupation

True evil hides cloaked in fine robes
Stealing our essence stealing our gold

Cowardly consistent authority defines
All of the problems look at the signs

Infested by maggots cockroaches hide
Can't take the light fear full inside

Confusion on purpose deeds done at night
Leading the mass's in fear full fright

Holly in hollicost religions true self
Justifying division no matter for wealth

Holly diver dark by design
Men bent on power drunk on its wine

Fighting frustration discontent
Anger brewing life's descent

Right where power breeds and grows
In the pit of each our souls

Listless life uninformed
Forcing us to conform

Oldest tricks in the book
Authority looking like a crook

Preaching freedom love and hope
Offering solution salvation dope

Church the cause and effect
Earth the victim no respect

Disposable trash lined banks
Once pure waters now have stanks

Spread your seed all the land
Dirty conscious dirt hand

Justified by your book
All those lives that's been took

Clear blue waters breathing life
Codependent husband wife

Jolting journey jarring truth
Egotistical path historic sleuth

Chasm growing as we speak
Willing victims misguided weak

Psychological terror on the rise
Can't be hidden from my eyes

Freedom starts from within
Free yourself from church's sin

They are guilty we are free
I love life it's meant to be

Discharge division and their fear
Quiet the mind own and steer

Old in memory old in power
Too much blood without shower

It's my body and my mind
Here to learn how I can shine

Burden barriers one two three
This is the number of your trinity

A theory squed perpatration
Power mad obliteration

Look in the mirror and be honest
What's looking back is it your fondest

Self image important but what's inside
Are you still hiding looking cross eyed

Detergent won't wash away all that pain
It's a commitment it don't take a brain

Open that heart live in the now
You don't need religion the self knows the how

Passed down and passed on everytime
Same old result conformity confined

Accordance to power manipulate the mass
High on itself smoking good grass

Don't believe me see if I care
I'll still be me because I dare

Compass guided purified
Open heart glorified

Destination the unknown
Searching for my lost home

Know it's here I'm not lost
I will find it no matter cost

Burried now millenium
Sensing some phenomenon

Surfacing in the now
Waking up in the wow

It's our turn something new
Cutting ties from feeling blue

Rock-n-roll smoke a bowl
Give me justice or dig my hole

Hands not tied behind my back
I climb the ladder out of wack

Come and go beyond the vail
Creations train creations rail

Are you the engine or caboose
Was your life of any use

What's the lessons what's be learnt
Is your heart burning or been burnt

Black and white or pastoral
Conformity or betrayal

Duelist in our nature
Tested daily building stature

Confused or clear still holding on
Finding purpose what's gone wrong

Tantalized the unknown
Lives inside me I call it home

You can't take what you can't see
Is why how I've come to be

Happy creed without greed

Affectionate vibe solar stride

Bringing hope without dope

Changing times stellar rhymes

Hold the light shine it bright

Confidence so intense

Soaring through sticky glue

Bread to win without sin

Catapult with a jolt

Captivate down to fate

Realize see through the lies

Patronize firey skies

Plug the hole bleeding soul

Catch the falling they will be balling

Body aching from the fall
Yes I know I've heard the call

Living in this paradigm
Not to worship but to shine

Is there anything I feel
That can make this all seem real

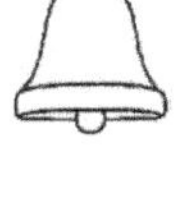

No deviation now
Straight ahead I plow

Many road blocks lie ahead
But I'm ready cuz I'm fed

Situations come and go
Some they never leave your soul

I'm just keeping up the trust
No more boarders go for bust

How could something so great cause so much pain
Don't know the reason plenty of blame

Tried to destroy me it didn't work
I'm calling you out your some kind of jerk

Knife to the back kick to the nuts
Go back to your old ways back to the sluts

Couldn't take my energy this I know
Couldn't control me so you had to go

Narcissist manipulator tried to feed
Energy vampire doing the deed

You never met anybody like me
I have real access because I am free

I'm not rolling over I won't be your rug
Never again will you get my hug

The end is the end no turning back
It's likely you'll burn out and maybe crack

Arch's arched out to be seen
Natures beauty dizzying

Our precious earth mother abundantly
Gives us all we'll ever need

Her heart beat beating in all that's here
Vibrant loving always near

A helping hand when we're down
Rising our vibration every town

Splendor glowing creations gift
Give her love and she will lift

Trust her glory will come back
Sovern creatures under attack

This abomination society
Is not right is not free

Conflicted in its every move
Conformity has found its groove

Never ending how I should live
Just one more false narrative

Tell me please what's life about
So confusing spinning out

How many more lessons how many more tries
I don't understand why tries turn to cries

Energy rising vibration bold
Why should I listen to what I am told

Where is the exit what is the plan
Cannot distinguish where I now am

Some foreign place this is not home
Why do these creatures talk with a phone

They can't be this lost no way no how
What's going on here I want to know now

Primitive in nature fighting with sticks
6000 years of building with bricks

Where is the vision what do I see
No one I meet is actually free

Losing control panic ensues
Just an illusion many a fools

Taught and instructed be in control
It's a trap one more dark hole

Of course the end leads to the grave
No one's coming; no one to save

We've saved ourselves when we shine
Become as one connected divine

Hostile acts name of God
Shame on you foolish squad

Men of honor led to die
Holly wars fire sky

Get a grip stop the trip
Guilt by association just the tip

Does the sun forget to rise

Do the stars forget to shine

Do the flowers forget to bloom

Does a river forget to flow

Do the bee's forget to pollinate

Do the birds forget to sing

Does a fish forget to swim

Do our hearts forget to love

Do the people forget to play

Does a touch forget to feel

Do the tears forget to weep

Do the eyes forget to see

Does the soul forget to grow

Without it we wouldn't know

Lost in translation spreading the blues
What will come next nothing to loose

Get off the couch change around things
Rid of the junk food start eating beans

What are you doing what is your fear
Contemplate nothing conformity clear

We are the one we have the power
Forget all the foolishness that's here in this hour

Fooled to conform believing in what
We all have a crack it's on our butt

New version is bitchen I cannot lie
Stop telling yourself why why why why

Free to explore any and all
Which door is next that's down this hall

Whatever stay in your fear
Eat on the couch drinking that beer

Recharged back at it again
Give me a moment so I can sin.

Laughing so hard my balls get a tingle
Shadow moment glad I'm still single

Testing the boundaries deciding for self
Boundless possibilities without a doubt

Barrel cooling time to reload
Nothing as it seems carry the load

Packaged as hope nice and neat
Wolves in sheeps clothing beating their meat

Laughing again ignorance prevails
Light up the internet pull out the nails

Provocative cunning distilling fine wine
Finding the willing rescued from swine

What about the pearl the one that don't exist
Is it really real the size of 20 fists

Why can no one find it maybe it wasn't time
Or did everyone stop looking forgetting the divine

What about the dragon and the unicorn
All we have now is T.V. and porn

Myth and legend a time long since forgotten
Reaching for some TP so I can wipe my bottom

Ancestual wisdom passing buried long ago
Now it's in the forefront here to let you know

Biting off the head spitting out the poison
Watch the fire burn after the explosion

Controls got to go it's been here too long
Hostage of emotions bitter nasty song

Like a weighs been lifted wait and see
What is meant meant for we

Quite the journey quite the ride
Highs and lows hope now to glide

Intuition listening brings me piece
Open heart love release

All the past melted away
It's my turn it's time to play

Hard to tell how high I've flown
But now I've landed now I'm home

Without baggage that held me back
True intentions sooth my back

Let's all listen to our heart song
Learn it live it to belong

Sleep at night means going home
A place I long for on my own thrown

Master creator skilled in love
Here to usher no false dove

Blocked from progress not no more
Keys to open any door

Diligent daring touched the fire
Open heart one desire

Understanding of our truth
Weights and measures seeking proof

Stagered weary forward trudge
Clearing poison and its sludge

Dictation present natural
It's the purpose of my soul

Essence gleaming portals clear
Aware existing near and dear

Not a minute goes by that I miss your smile
I'd swim an ocean walk a million a mile

Every breath every hour
Heart is broken no more power

I take credit I hurt you so
Now I'm lonely wet and cold

Maybe a chance you'll take me back
Please I'm begging heart attack

I did not know we were so good
I was stupid a no good hood

My promise is I'll be knid
Patient loving all the time

Your my queen I love you so
Take me back so we can grow

Bringing smiles with my work
Quite the bennie quite the perk

You want laughter you want strain
How about anything insane

Rock-n-roll may heal your soul
But smoking crack will make you wack

Jesus freaks they seem so proud
Not seeing what's inside the cloud

Appreciation for salvation
Earth lies wounded degragation

Justifying ever move
Missing pieces out of grove

Manipulation far and wide
Power winning the divide

Brought from Europe to this land
Is not worth its weight in sand

Hitting homeruns every time
With the greatness of divine

Oneness flowing through these veins
Healing power take the reigns

Intuition of a saint
I see through you what you ain't

Talk so Godly scriptures read
Justifying all the dead

It's my power I recall
Responsible for my own ball

Picnic lunch in my basket
There will never be a casket

Entombed in brilliant light so bright
Eager resting through the night

Anxiety has no hold
This is fear I got gold

When hell becomes real
It's time to heal

Your answers are inside
That's where they hide

They're not in a book
Where hell is the crook

Divinity's been divided
On purpose can't hide it

Chaos confines
Ignorance defines

Everything opposite
Without greed and profit

Brimming on hope
Salvations on dope

Drunk on its power
Take a cold shower

Hold your own hand
Its time learn to stand

No one listening standing around
Thumb in the ass look what I've found

A presence in self without any book
Intuition that's mine society once took

Guided for sure answering the why's
All of the things I once despised

Not right not wrong just not truth
Spiritually manipulated look around for the proof

Warship to avoid means fear
Ignorance flows into each ear

What we've forgotten
Is that we’re not rotten

Flawed from the birth straight from the source
What's the excuse must be one of course

Religion is stupid it's lost its need
It feeds on the people greedy in deed

Suicide I see it soon
Maybe on the next full moon

Art of deception clever indeed
Filling a want getting a need

Destroying the unknown wiping the seed
Tools of the evil bleeding with greed

Seizing control purifying the lands
Pillage and plunder with both hands

Ambitious in blood whatever it takes
Off with the heads burnt at the stakes

Righteous in God out of their mouth
Cross's appear on each of its house

Transmuting time no better than before
Same trap for the victims mass's in horror

Upright still walking on two legs
Eager in ignorance hopelessly begs

For something new steral in truth
Look in your heart I am the proof

Egg shell foundation built on bones
Chilling history throwing stones

Power thwarting freedoms trail
Greedy criminals belong in jail

Tricky tactics clever scheme
Barbarism of esteem

Stripped down naked without choice
Hear me now hear my voice

Fear full falsehoods fairytales
Serving only land locked whales

Property barons royalty
Time has come to pay the fee

Signs of private no such thing
Programs to hide everything

Eager beavers build a dam
Hiding history of the land

No one can run no one can hide
Rise up face that fear inside

Condescending critic take a seat
In the back row and beat your meat

I'm come you go
Not down with that negative flow

Take your book and go back
Find a dealer buy your crack

Truth be know your like mold
Fungus growing smelling old

Stinky trash smelly can
Fat and ugly white no tan

Slaves of burden others greed
Human condition withered seed

Drink some water healthy meal
Respect your body maybe heal

Wash my mouth out with some soap
I am not a hopeless dope

Precious childhood youth
Without any real truth

Dialect demeans
Giving up on dreams

Parental strive of the hive

Nitch dug in controlled from within

Scarf to hid the scars worries in the jars

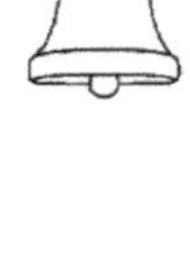

Tence to earn a buck conformity must suck

Emotions on the sleeve begging momma please

Love has run away doesn't wanna stay

Who 'yah gonna blame maybe in the name

Prestigious pedestal growing up a toll

Whatever gotta go
See 'ya next time at the show

Beholden to a book written by a crook

Half and partial lies conformity denies

Manipulate the mass's burnt covered in ashes

Dead end conversation mental masturbation

Disturbing acts of terror history its barer

Poisonous thorny spikes visionary kikes

Pedestal built on ground that isn't very sound

Talking points so weak besides what feeds the weak

Squawking to the end not time to pretend

As above so below pack your bags it's time to go

Pride honor respect code of conduct
Obligation subject and topic

Honor the heroes are they really
Tools of war that is silly

Respect the machine that keeps us free
Never a time no one can see

Pride in a land conquered and stolen
Fashion a noose I know the bolan

Promises broken rewrite the books
Back of one man crooks with hooks

Can of worms beans been spilt
Temple building many kilt

Obligation now I sigh
Brothers always while we cry

Many a martyrs it took to get here
Seeming senseless not always clear

Oppressors pressing down on our breasts
Suffocation every last breath

Misled conditioned talked down and lies
Never ending false narratives no surprise

Condoning behavior societal norm
Take this drug it will make you feel warm

Never an answer opinions galore
Pharmaceutical empire everyone's whore

Diagnosis behavior treat it with drugs
Victimization cowardly thugs

So many degrees so little brains

Out in the desert holding on
What was real now is gone

The missing parts that freed my soul
Confident steering towards my goal

Inner peace to guide my way
Child like seeming likes to play

Embracing each moment that I'm here
Whispered teachings in each ear

Open to a brand new way
Bound to cosmic never sway

Insight gleaning ever clear
Lost and lonely now I'm here

Where is here not quite sure
In the cosmos bright and pure

Appeasing power virtue less guilt
Empire building from the hilt

Authority intimidation
Broken backs every nation

New paint over old canvas
We are divine how can we stand this

Respecting one element that makes us sick
Forgetting the self blinding trick

Psychology nonsense void of real answers
Just like doctors studying cancers

Societal cancer maybe the root
Separation from source simply put

Spirituality is for the brave
Religion for those who want to be saved

Go ahead figure it out
I wouldn't write it if I had any doubt

Most call it progress I call it greed
Influencing power to feed it's need

Codependency created one mans blood
Misguided intentions from under a hood

No love in power no love in guilt
Shame is the poison that has been built

Preaching nonsense from its perch
Authoritarism stripping back from berch

Cloked in madness poised to fail
Here's your spike not a nail

Challenge me and find out
I'm a master without a doubt

Shady suckers fall in line
Drunk on fear and lots of wine

Forgotten is our truer self
Kind and caring better health

A ripened fruit sweet and soft
Giving meaning never lost

Heart still growing ever strong
Sleep has lasted far too long

Awake and free no strings attached
From the fear I am detached

Compassion flowing no compromise
Karmatic collusion big surprise

Bathed in sunlight washed in sand
Now it time to heal the land

Us inhabitants of this place
I've heard it called the human race

Find respect find some pride
Get off your ass and get outside

Watching the rest becoming my best

Flail in folly no resemblance of wholly

Pissed off in pain trapped in the rain

Conformity confounds same old sounds

*Bitter and dead f*cks with your head*

Only the heart will set you apart

There is a need to grow this seed

We are not livin until we start given

We are the power this is our hour

The church is the weed we own our own seed

It needs us to exist ignorance precists

Glory to the one not martyrs son

Religion and division it's done well
Prophets speak of a place called hell

Dose of fear for mankind
Casting shadows on divine

Burp the baby it's not well
And change its diaper what's that smell

Dead rat in a trap met its fate
Uninspired and lifeless wicked state

Out of breath going down
Every city ever town

Wait and see whats to come
Shiver bumps keep me numb

Don't tell me I didn't tell you so
The church's power has stole your soul

Operation conformity
Stolen what we were meant to be

Just when hope seems to fade away
A brilliant vision comes my way

A touching gesture lifts me up
Natures beauty fills my cup

Alive and healing my best friend
With me 'till the unknow end

Gracious giving all she is
Surrigate mother lives to live

Timing perfect giving strength
Not always easy but I thank

Clouded covered in her womb
Spacious plenty lots of room

Pouring passion lifted grace
Ever present smiling face

Mental anguish because we're sick
Society pressure like a brick

Confusing misguided all about wealth
Disease ridden perception not in good health

Backward and twisted moral surprise
Each time I get here each time I rise

Above the fog clear in sight
Message bearing patiently right

Hostil intentions I'm aware
I'm protected without a care

With or against matters not
Not my plan not my knot

Mine's untied and dangling long
Confident I sing along

Be your best and just try
Ignore opinion old shall die

I am now numb did I just succumb

Lost in the dream passion esteem

Carried over the line one final sign

Waiting to fly permanent high

Desire fulfilled love been revealed

Steadfast the tease humming like bees

Found from within the ultimate win

Gimmie a chance to express how I feel
Get on my cloud spin the big wheel

Give thanks of knowledge the air that we breathe
The sun the moon the earth and the trees

Created by all for us to enjoy
Live out the dream shameless in joy

Peaceful and present each moment each day
Concious of trueness each act we display

Abundance of love vibrating about
Is this the heaven that christians tout

Pureness of heart lively and fun
How 'bout a walk or go for a run

How 'bout you focus on what you conceal
The things that you think the things that you feel

Wrapped up so tight so serious in vain
Better be careful not to blow up your brain

Courage to fight strength to stay
Living in piece each passing day

Enjoying the life that I've been givin'
Free in this bounty like my own heaven

Caught a real break not quiet sure why
Pain from my past taught me to cry

Now I have come now is our time
Light lives in darkness let it shine

Bottom of the 9th here comes the sign
Ready I wait this one is mine

Here comes the curve and there it goes
Out of the park into the sholes

Crowd is all cheering miracle it seems
Trusting my training living the dream

Rectify common sense
No more dollars only cents

Tabou teasing tempting time
Teachers teaching nursery rhyme

Despite dogma doing deeds
Washing terror over its seeds

Nasty notes knowing news
Unleash panic sing the blues

Big blue balls being bought
Let the people smoke their pot

Innocence injured internally
Go away and let us be

Control craving constant care
Boasting bravely dead ass stair

Ditch the pitch it's only lies
I've seen the truth it's in my eyes

Beat down but fighting for what I deserve
Wishing my life had not seen this curve

I may be down but don't count me out
Life is a mystery without a doubt

Thread one more needle eye of the storm
Life is worth living why I was born

Asking for courage strength to move on
Head above water turbulence gone

Send me my peace sing me my song
Let my heart open so I can move on

Wish on a star see my own grace
Stop pointing fingers and finish the race

Hold onto that child don't let it go
Learn from her pain then you will know

What is balance what does this mean
I feel like the shavings from a machine

Pulling me somewhere to and fro
What's going on I do not know

This should be easy it's only life
Hopelessness growing cuts like a knife

Upright in courage growing tall in strength
What's wrong with my mind I think I might faint

Actions are doing thoughts are pretend
Only our actions matter in the end

Where is the blueprint how to find grace
What's going on with human race

One more deep breath feeling the still
Another mountain or just a hill

Stepping in rhythm my own cadence clear
Never again will I live in fear

In the silence
I still hear the violence

Make it go away
I can't take another day

Free me from this pain
Too much pressure too much strain

Liberate my truth
Give your blessings to our youth

Stop the hands of time
Be the one and let us shine

Walk me down your path
Keep me clear of evils rath

Permeate my essence
Keep me from life's sentence

Help me with my mission
I hope there's nothing missing

Labeling lunacy to define
Conditioned value not divine

Statistically speaking scientific crap
Laying the ground work for another trap

Produced and controlled wow so smart
Separation in the heart

Blocked intelligence educated fools
Science the apple you the tools

I know you wanna save me cuz that's what you know
But this is my planet I run the show

Power of creation lives in my bones
Don't need a computer don't need a phone

Stand back watch and learn
Tide is high and about to turn

Que ball in hand after a scratch
Run out the table finish the match

Planning the win with a new spin

Practice and poised playing with toys

Get right and stay or get out of the way

The jokes on you cuz you did not pursue

Hardly worth laughing conformity's staffing

Eager to steal under the spiel

Tongue twister tries blabbing its lies

Persecute the weak power does seek

Same old story without glory

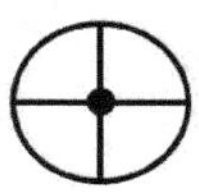

Riding a train for the insane

Windows of shadow can't see out
Innocent screaming horrified they shout

Darkness conductor full throttle ahead
Brain wash the weak manipulate the head

False obligation miracle narrations
Staining the people staining all nations

Divisive behavior separation quite clear
Twisted intentions constantly fear

Not of my doing not of my plan
Not of the love not of the hand

Above as below what a line
Witness the miracle witness divine

Never tired never weak
Ever present ever meek

Shattered and torn just like porn

Crucifixion thee affliction

Muddy water on the plotter

Covert mission always fishin'

Black out opps dirty cops

Holly shit like a zit

Terrorize blackened eyes

Google mad so dumb sad

Electric blind does define

Pathetic posture always costs her

Altered preception thee deception

Suffication strangle hold
Never growing always told

Blocked and backed up feaverish
Same old meal same old dish

Deflection darting subject changed
Always wearing bondage chains

Obligation wrong in sight
Looking for the next fight

Out to pasture no more milk
Covered in a fine ass silk

Deception casting playing role
Keep us stupid steel our soul

Alarming witness siering light
Breathless breathing through the night

Teather anchored cosmic wealth
Healthy eating move in stealth

Afixiation smothered in guilt
Wrong end of the sword hold the hilt

Brimstone burning oh so hot
Conditioning ignorance causing rot

Blasfamous rumors haratics of power
Easy to spot bigots devour

Posture poisoning preseption squed
Vomiting lectures sounding crued

Licking the sack filled stolen gold
Beholden to power watched it unfold

Greed compromising all in some name
Never responsible relient on blame

Absent and tardy separated and distant
Controlling the people always persistent

Heard enough call my bluff

Smoke up your skirt it's gonna hurt

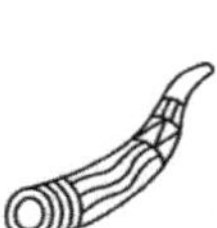

What's your past full of hurt
Contaminated soil foul dirt

Toxic persons robbing vibe
Brainwashed victims of the hive

Buzzing breeding ignorant
Stealing all that's innocent

Egregious journey twists and turns
Leave behind all that burns

Tripping zombies sucking souls
Blinded bastards callous tolls

Dense divided wholly hell
Ding-dong ping-pong smash that shell

Kneejerk handjob oh my God
Rest assured I did sawed

To damn easy cracking up
Spilling over is my cup

Committed to truth tested by lies
Hear my calling realize

Surrendered surface serenity subsides
Silly sanctions suicide

Trail blazing soaring about
Pouters pouting dreams without

Tedious talking no real point
Out of step painful joint

Wishful thinking gone arry
Pesky rodents do rely

Firehose wash it down
Quell the ugly in your town

Springs for cleaning and rebirth
Do a solid save the earth

Watch the stars feel the trees
Hear the birds and the bees

We can do this defeat the grift
Loving hearts our true gift

Counterfeit creation one man's life
Justifying massive strife

Dabbling dip wits daring dogs
Holding mass's slaughtering hogs

Robes of darkness imagery
Not how life was meant to be

Golden wishes solution stained
Terroristic all insane

Temple builders wholly grail
Sick and sad behind the vail

Low vibration how it feeds
Supporting evil darkened deeds

Ten fold coming back to end
Pardon the interruption time to send

Elegant angles primitive pie
Ancient traditions sights the sky

Inner knowing justice and truth
Standing strong tarnished youth

It's our time fill the void
Greatest honor can't be annoyed

Fallen angles of the light
Strong we carry humanity plight

Downloads heavy on our backs
Worriers defend never attack

Hasty thoughs disappear
Vision focus becoming clear

Tantalizing wisdom flows
From our heads to our toes

With ease moving to and fro
Love and guidance always flow

Explanation don't make sense
Grappling gripping to past tense

Same old shit different day
Feeding the herd rotten hay

Keep um strung out at a cost
Emotional drugs is the boss

Preacher pretending they you friend
Same old poison same old end

Stifel growth stay in line
Lashings coming twisted twine

Delirious downward angst anoints
Sick and greedy sucking points

Bridge to nowhere dead end street
Paralized wheelchair seat

Dereliction of duty timing off
Backfire eminent unhealthy cough

Playing the game I see your cards
Remind me of a bunch of tards

Intimidation that won't work
Validation like a jerk

Old ass tools lookin' fools

Doxing dodes blanks for loads

One more job who's left to rob

Arbitrary quite contrary

Insolation from infestation

Huddled in the past existing in the pain
Conductors of the greed full throttle on the train

Buried evil realm darkness at the helm

Sucking out the soul poison in its bowl

Birthright baby you and me
Light your own candle and you will see

Heart song sings angle wings
Passion flowing through all things

Lifted higher everyday
Love to laugh sing and play

Led to proof honor pride
Seatbelt off bumpy ride

Worth it all severed ties
Even though each day I cry

Forever this heart pure and true
Be your best don't be blue

One foot in front of the other
No more hiding under the cover

Perpetuated quick sand trap
Not gonna take this load of crap

Eager yearning priceless dreams
No more torture no more screams

Victimhood baby bottle fed
Woke beginning led by fed

Crossfire crazy power stands
Handcuffs belong on the hands

Traitor inside every room
No mop will do or a broom

Messy Marvin Lionel
Someone please erase the smell

Middle of nowhere no map to get home
Ignorance preaching false from its thrown

Brutal in content conformity rules
Blinding the bastards ruling the fools

Vital in sucking all that it can
Energy demon each with a bran

One of the herd stripped of content
Martyr division with evil intent

I see what they're taking see what's been took
Long standing religion imperial crook

One generation all it will take
Bite off the head of the poisonous snake

The universe is calling open up
Let its light fill your cup

Cup half empty cup half full
Foolish gibberish bad card to pull

Playing with a full deck I got flow
Let me show you what you do not know

Cautious no more obliterate
Dismantling narratives causing such hate

Pendulum swinging time to get right
Reboot your mind let your heart feel the light

Citizens of the multiverse rise and awake
We are here to cause a shake

Sward in sheath tongue on fire
Universe awaits all desire

Rock-n-roll fills my soul
We the one don't cha know

Lasting lineage DNA
Pleasures mine now lets play

Up beat willing helpful and kind
Lifting persons with these rhymes

Eager beaver broken mold
Not afraid to be bold

Heart set free limits none
Should anyone have this much fun

Desire driven invisioning
Always clearing always spring

Dedication to my craft
Floating lonely on hand made raft

Continous confidence passionate
Freed myself from the net

Brought to awareness dispensation
Who allowed this in our nation

Sorrow in the sadness
Tears are never endless

Disrespect in all forms
Separation it conforms

Serenading lies
Knowing wrong despise

Power gone astray
Corruption only way

Distant memories
Shaking at my knees

Perforate the mask
Promising a task

Guided by the heart
Let your journey start

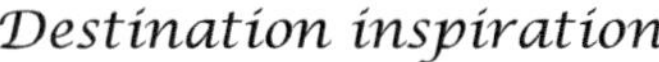

Destination inspiration

Whatever it takes
Without any breaks

Bread to be kind
Not triangular blind

Presence aware
Reality's despair

Melancholy prepairs
For all the stairs

Shaken not stured
Vision not blurred

Ascending so high
I think I can fly

Customized crown
Brilliant not brown

We are the one
Start having fun

Firm foundation shaky ground
Conformity causes altered sound

Mixed vibration unseen illusion
Separation from the union

Energy restriction inflicting pain
What's the point for the drain

Power of course silly horse

Written words toilet turds

Limitation foul stagnation

Imagination's where it's at
Pack a bag grab a hat

Learn the lessons be yourself
Let opinions not affect your health

It's our world take it back
From elitists children smoking crack

Out on a ledge this life I pledge

Rumors abound negative sound

Entrapped in falsehoods stealing our goods

Mask wearing clown bringing us down

Birds of a feather sick from its teather

Cut to the chase breaking our race

No one is better all are together

Hostage no more life is no bore

Kind and brave don't need to be saved

Holicoast symptom professional victim

Warrior poet and I know it

Proud to fight any day or night

Starlight skating on thin ice
Danger danger don't be enticed

Aggravation spilling out
From a bottle baby's pout

Here's a tissue dry your tears
Society living in its own fears

Oppressed through negativity
Never wholesome never free

Our dignity comes from within
Let your love feel again

Mysterious moving intense at times
Why I've come to write these rhymes

Foot of God not the hand
Religious ruins promised land

Boarders slicing up creation
Divided people divided nation

Doing its job with intention
Critical mass pay attention

Pendulum swinging time for change
No room for ugly or deranged

Window pain three finger lid
Keep it quite keep it hid

Envy eating jealous juice
Haters hating liars loose

Light of courage cunning strength
Winning battles free of stink

Wings spread wide soaring high
Back to my home in the sky

What's this world all about
Why do humans scream and shout

Forgotten purpose led astray
Dream of nothing as they pray

Ostentatious heads so big
No comprehension what's the gig

Waking wasted all spun out
Game is over it was a route

Choice removed free will gone
Obligation just a pawn

Dead man's diary impression clear
Stamp of shame and of fear

Care so much don't care at all
Collecting strength for the fall

Push or shove how 'bout the boot
To the news you like to toot

Your own horn annoying sound
Life thats lived under ground

Soil pleading for the light
To give birth without freight

Hollowed ground soil unturned
Signals sent from all who yearned

Captured captive in own skin
Time for healing to begin

Boxed ambition storage full
Grab the horns of the bull

Baby steps will do at first
To discover what you can birth

Imagination running free
Deep roots planted like a tree

Obey and pray conformity ritual
Power knows it cuz it's critical

Hey Peter heard you got keys
Bring them to me I'm asking please

Time for a cure mixing it up
Fill love to the rim let it spill from your cup

Gracious and kind peaceful and calm
No need to create another bomb

Eager to learn heart is a burn

Ratchet me higher fill this desire

Make what was sent eliminate lent

Rock all the cores get rid of the sores

Expose the dimension I rarely mention

Dig up the krath and bring back my path

Hold on for the ride in us does hide

How 'bout an opinion nope psych
Here's a middle finger now take a hike

To many times blocking this path
Our karmas done it's taken a bath

Maybe I'll miss you don't really care
Now I stand up exposing my pair

Be upset fine with me
I need a life happy and free

Keep on worrying keep casting guilt
It's your justification that you have built

Conformity fault obvious
But no more of that bliss

You keep going got my own course
Been nice to know you this of course

Seduced by salvation drunk on a book
Not understanding what has been took

To arrogant to admit maybe wrong
Deaf to the words I hear in my song

I don't read can barely spell
But I went to this place religion calls hell

Stayed there and fought for all I was worth
The reward was given all of this earth

Metiphysical speaking hard to be sure
But negative emotions were never a cure

So I cautiously create a roadmap of sorts
To purge the negative from our shorts

Yes short comings outbursts and such
Sort of like replacing a slipping clutch

It will be work but think of the new
The new is found in each of you

New found love an inner child
Under the chaos out in the wild

Your choice stay addicted
I'm free not afflicted

Ashes to ashes dust to dust
Power and control can't resist lust

To much temptation alluring scent
Drunk on power narrative bent

Trapped by emotions psychologically dead
To the gift we all have is what I said

Our greatest strength the love we share
Stolen away by terrorists who dare

To convenient never made sense
Salvation sickness so intense

Powers chain abrasive ways
Creepy pastors lost in haze

Two lumps of fear one of hope
Righteous behavior is a joke

Imprint impression from child birth
Conformity's vision to control the earth

Happy and healthy without the laws
Those of religion and its cause

Cutting its nose off despite its face
Never losing control of our race

Speaking of God while leaving a trail
Turn to violence and empail

Prime example of madness prevails
Religion in general belongs in jails

Do to it what it does to us
Thieves of innocence built on lust

True nature in history again and again
Led by the nose to conquer in sin

Not so fortunate the ones of chosen
Ice water veins maybe your frozen

Professional victims watch your back
The lives of your ancestors are super wack

Gifts are collected and plenty of gold
Slaves of the system evil is sold

Kindness for granted not no more
Here's my foot out the door

All the energy all the support
How did I end up in your court

Judge has judged and I don't care
I deserve better than an ugly stare

Lessons learned never again
No more narcists will get in

Sanctuary sacred deep within
Woven fabric beneath the skin

Love me hate me not my place
Too much sadness on each face

Society's pitfalls controlling adults
Not willing to admit its many faults

AI science what's been warned
Evils madness sorta like porn

You're right I will never stop
Not until change is at the top

Sorrow from the guilt welling up again
What regret is this wiping out my grin

Intuition tool compromised
Bringing tear drops to my eyes

Superstitions sound like fear
Wrong direction crystal clear

Not of light but the dark
Like your car is stuck in park

Introspection take some time
Put the cork back on that wine

Get 'um when they young poison the seed
Someday they'll come back when they feel the need

Predictable behavior inspiration lost
Frigid essence cold as frost

Bewildered herd of blind faith
Stuck in slavery nowhere safe

Dissatisfaction discontent
Justification smelly scent

Ok I'll be nice
Next time maybe pay the price

Pride not pity unconditional love
Heart space protected from above

Army of angels by my side
Keeping me safe from those who lied

Walking with destiny sleeping with fate
Gotta say it feels quite great

Ever present in my mind
From where we come and our design

Comfort zone on the rise
Come on really what's the prize

Love and laughter bring it on
What's the point of what's been sawn

Stillness feeds that inner child
Could not break me still am wild

Not for all but the some
Better than the years of numb

Expectation been let down
Selfish reason as I drown

Over my head feeling uneasy
I don't think my thoughts are sleezy

Tried to work out reasonable
But my plate is to dumb full

Earie sense of what could be
Who put mushrooms in my tea

Tactful tactic what's been tried
But the purpose has no eyes

Standing steady on my own
Roots reach deep into the ground

Never never has revealed
After layers have been pealed

Always fun can't hold back
I think the planet has gone wack

Travelers far and wide
Who seek your guidance from inside

Our time has come the time is now
It's our mission to do the how

Approach the world stand with love
Courageously battle strength from above

Creation calling the many volunteers
Conscience cleared without fears

Command is free will do what's right
Towers be falling to our delight

No more constant threat or confusing lies
Time for truth to materialize

Individual freedom is our beginning and end
Stop at nothing don't pretend

Join me set your party free
Be everything that you can be

Leave the negative where it belongs
So it won't hold you in its throngs

Play your part be enriched
Stop living the life of a bitch

Stop the toil end the pain
Leave conformity and its restrain

Paint your own picture canvas clean
Watch your own movie star in every scene

Get ambitious motivate
Loral resting aint so great

Strive for better everyday
Don't forget to laugh and play

Adult living what a joke
Expecting respect opinion broke

Don't expect what's not deserved
Go back to the hole control serves

This way and that pushed and pulled
In this place to be schooled

Forgotten why we've come
Misguided by the scum

Railroaded out of spite
Trampled on our every right

Reputation in our face
Martyr model to save the race

Terrified to stand up
Here it goes to spill my cup

This river flows and can't be stopped
No matter who's waiting at the top

Not a waver not a shake
Pitch fork holding to slay the snake

Count the excuses justified
Trapped in conformity and its lies

Terrified in silence anxiety ridden
If you only knew what was hidden

Greatest con job of them all
Leading society to its fall

Barron landscape spiritually corrupt
One grain of sand in each cup

Privately morning stricken with grief
What is the problem what's the beef

Course correction possible
End the suffering of the soul

Bound to blathering no escape
Altered by two headed snake

Easy does it just hold on
Persuade the ass up off the john

In the toilet where it belongs
Negativities of all ding-dongs

Callous clerics rich in power
Collecting riches every hour

Old in trick fooling fools
Not equipped with right tools

Bearing witness once again
History repeats one on the chain

Much destine can't explain
Can't refrain from insane

Carried cargo with embargo
Dark old show without glow

Tomorrow's path in yesteryears rath
Guarded truth is my proof

It's always a choice how we react
It's not okay to hold back on wack

It's always a choice how we feel
It's never ok to not heal

Circumstances good and bad
The past is over it's a had

The now is all's we've ever had
To prove that we have learned from bad

Unbecoming behaves from lack
It's a symptom of the wack

Dark descended from the past
Keeping hostage false egos last

Just one spark just one act
Can change our lives help drain the sack

Festering frustration discontent
It's our power alone not for rent

Given all's we ever needed
Is the message I've been hidded

Ask yourself who you be
Don't let labels control thee

Perry poison ozzing out
Salvation secret what's in doubt

Prophets power held in high
Most of witch is powers lie

It's our connection from where we come
Religion is what makes us numb

Emotionally bamboozled cut to chase
Psychologically corrupted in your face

Haters be hatin' lovers be lovin
It's a choice to get free from the oven

Break free if you wanna be

Stay in denial in the last mile

I'm living proof each has a truth

Esoteric in nature light is our future

Ghostly for most I stand at my post

Message in rhymes gonging the chimes

False in façade scaring through God

Whiplash of betrail blood in its trail

Cross in hand cowards stand

Narcissistic go ballistic

Teaching moment seek atonement

Karmatic clue feeling blue

Heart space closed dully glows

Trafficking pain is insane

Justice revealed emotions healed

Don't need book of the crook

Tampered power here's your tower

Obligations far and wide
Separation meant to divide

Loyality through frosted lens
Broken back from the bends

Misplaced trust respect not deserved
Take a look at to whom you may serve

Son or father rest in peace
Who's the head of the beast

Manipulation of true self
Cut down young to prevent true wealth

Gluttonous struggle persistency persuades
Frying the eggs that have been laid

Scorched earth approach molten fire pond
I need a break and a good yawn

Searing secret power don't care
It has no low to where it may dare

Thirsty hungry free my soul
Stop the pain and its toll

Heal me love me show yourself
Bring me guidance bring me health

Turn my path from the cliff
Give me traction so I don't slip

Thread my needle quite the storm
Bring me true love instead of porn

Carry me hold me keep me safe
Give me strength to face this faith

Serenade my inner child
Happy loving free and wild

Clear my path erase my stain
Lift me clear of the vain

Detonate the wicked lies
Hold your candle to their eyes

Test me try me make sure I'm true
Nothing ever could replace you

Natural order circular vibe
Triangles have too much to hide

Responsible for what we put out
Do you want love or do you want doubt

Do you want healing do you want grace
Set your intention move at your pace

Brutally honest humming in tune
Existing in truth enjoying the moon

Replenished and healthy full to the rim
No looking back fear cannot win

Ripples of goodness loving and kind
Get with the program or get left behind

Paradoxal pressure valve
Interdimensional to create and solve

Each our truth why we here
Don't let power pierce your pure

TO MY FRIEND PETER B.

The sacred heart knows its mind
The wounded soul will leave you blind

Starving from salvation
Salvation from what
A scary place created by some nut

Well I'm not scared I have no fear
And yes I've drunk plenty of beer

Conformity kills me I will say
It's all around me everyday

Individual sovereignty is where it's at
Spiritually awareness sly like a cat

9 lives to few more like a thousand
Stirring inside heart beat arousin

Intuition on point leading the way
Chaft from the stock cutting down hay

Smiling and grinning cuz I got flow
Dimensional travel now I must go